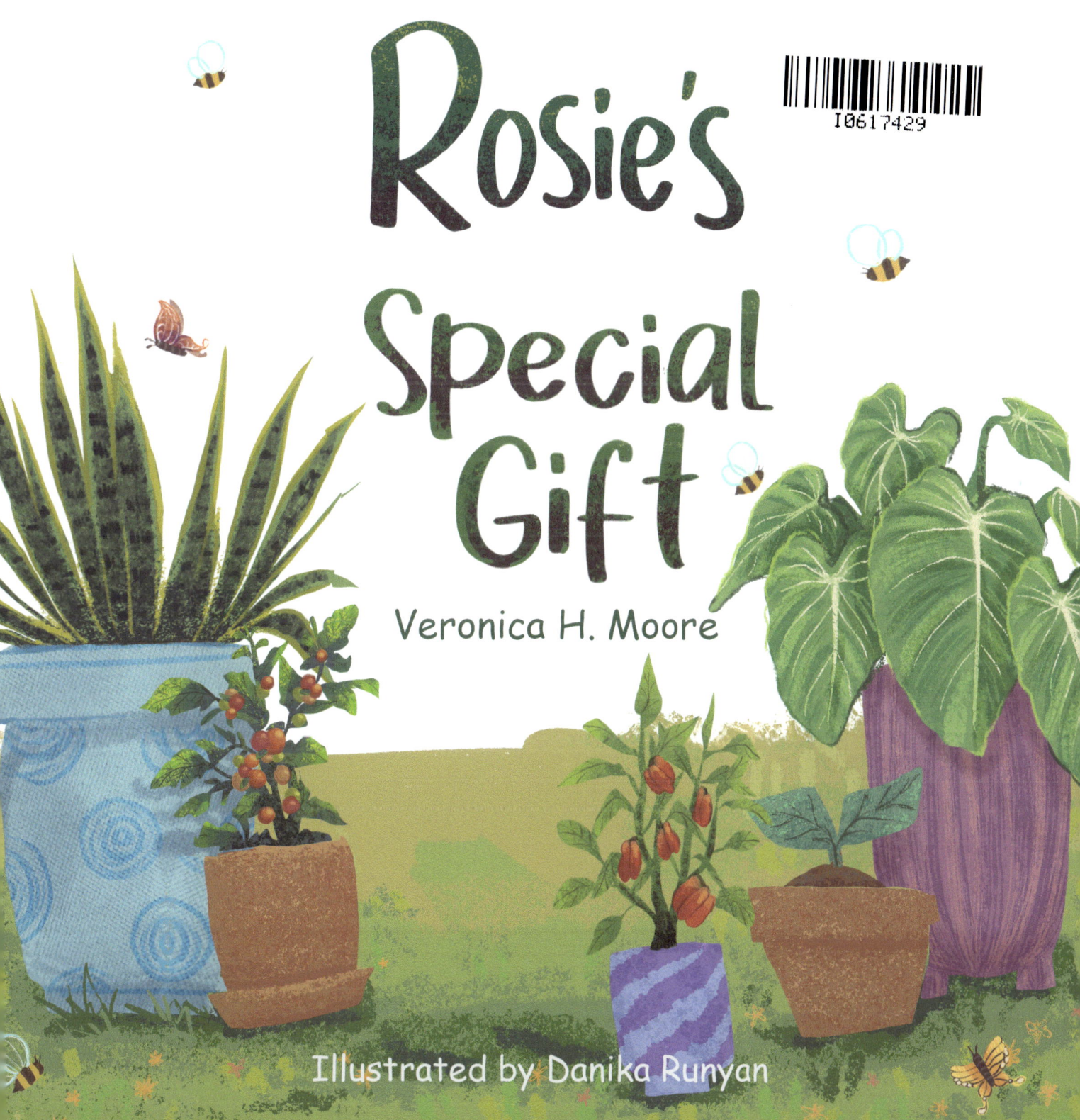

Rosie's Special Gift

Veronica H. Moore

Illustrated by Danika Runyan

This book is inspired by the author's connection to nature at a young age through her mother's teachings on how to grow food and take care of plants. The story is sentimental. What started out as a piece of children's literature highlighting the relationship between Veronica and her daughter quickly turned into an ancestral revelation of the lineage of caring for plants that is being passed down to others. We hope that Rosie's Special Gift will find its place of inspiration in your home and life as you plant, water and watch your seeds grow!

Text © 2023 Veronica H. Moore Illustrations © Danika Runyan
ISBN - 979-8-9892074-0-4 (paperback) ISBN - 979-8-9892074-1-1 (hardcover)
ISBN: 979-8-9892074-2-8 (ebook) LCCN: 2023918901

Leaf & Vine Books are available at special discounts when buying in bulk or for educational use.
For details, please contact us at leafandvinebooks@gmail.com or authorveronicahmoore@gmail.com

Rosie lives in a house on the hill. Inside her home there are lots of plants.

Big plants and small plants-all in different shades of green. Some even have fun shapes and textures!

Rosie loves to help her mom with the plants in their home. Watering them is her favorite thing to do because she knows plants need water and light to grow.

Rosie's mom always says, "Growing plants is a lot of work, but it's also a lot of fun!" One day while watering and misting plants,

Rosie decided to practice counting along the way. " 1, 2, 3... 8, 9, 10...

23, 24, 25... 48, 49, 50... Wow, so many!"

Rosie knew her mom loved plants and she was curious to know why. One day, while in the garden, she asked her mom, "Mommy, why do you love plants so much?"

"Well Rosie, plants are living things just like you and I. They teach us many lessons such as responsibility, patience, and giving to others. They also make people happy and this is what I love about them the most.

Plants clean the air we breathe in, provide food for us to eat, and make the inside of our homes beautiful."

When I was a little girl just like you, I would watch Grandma D take care of the plants in our home and in the garden. I was her little helper!

She showed me how to harvest the tomatoes, cucumbers, and peppers when they were ready for us to eat and share with others. I had so much fun helping her.

Grandma D shared her love for the earth with me, which is why I share the same things with you, Rosie."

Rosie was amazed at all that plants can do.
Everyday, Rosie's mom checks on their
houseplants and garden to make sure
everything is growing healthy and strong!
Rosie watches her with great
curiosity and always has
a new question to ask.

Her mom shares fun facts about them to show Rosie just how exciting learning about plants can be.

Rosie's mom loves teaching others about plants. She even gives them out as gifts to the people in the neighborhood and to those she loves.

When Rosie returns to school, it will be her turn to share for show-and-tell. The assignment was for everyone to bring an item that helped them feel happy.

Rosie had a great idea!

Rosie decided to bring in one of her plants to show her friends. Because she remembered plants can make other people happy too, she wanted to give her teacher and classmates a houseplant of their own!

Rosie wanted to pick out the perfect plant for her school friends.

So, she asked her mother if they could take a trip to the plant nursery on the weekend.

After looking around the nursery, Rosie ran up to a plant with dark and light green and yellow heart shaped leaves.

Philodendron Brazil

She handed the plant to her
mother and said, "This is the one!
I want everyone in my class to have
this plant!"
"Great choice," said Rosie's
mother. "I believe they will love it!"

When Rosie returned to school on Monday, she was very excited to share her special item for everyone to see.

The item Rosie brought was a houseplant her mother gave her when she was 3 years old. It was a special plant to Rosie and had grown very big.

After telling the story of her plant, Rosie shared with her classroom friends that she had a gift for each of them. Rosie walked over to her classroom cubby and grabbed the ten beautiful plants she brought to school that day.

Rosie said to her teacher and classmates, "I chose this plant for each of you to keep. Plants make me happy, and I hope they make you happy too!"

The End

Dedicated To

Mom - To the Matriarch who started it all. I couldn't imagine life without the special gift of growing green things that you taught me at a very tender age. I promise to keep the message of plant therapy alive in your honor.

To my daughter Hunter - you were the guiding light that sparked my desire to pour into the lives of children through literature. Thank you for cheering mommy on as an author and thank you for the naming of the main character, Rosie.

To my husband Quartez - thank you for continuing to support my artistic expression. This project of healing was everything I needed to tap into a new level. You always bring it out of me.

To the readers - May your hearts be touched forever in knowing that Plants are Therapy.

I love plants because...

Plants teach me about...

I want to share a plant with...

My garden and plant wishlist:

Veronica H. Moore is a celebrated educator, trainer, facilitator, children's book author and entrepreneur, who is determined to positively reshape the way children engage in social and emotional expression through the art of plant care and growing food. With an upbringing that Included gardening and taking care of houseplants, Veronica knows the effects and benefits that nature has on our lives.

Becoming a mother sparked Veronica's interest in children's literature. Wanting to see and promote characters that resembled her family's experience in nature was the main inspiration of her journey to authorship. She is an advocate of children's literature representing and promoting BIPOC characters as a main focal point. Her books published by Leaf & Vine Books are based in social & emotional learning and can be used as a tool both inside and outside of learning spaces. Veronica's work is often described as sentimental, warm and inviting.

When not writing, Veronica enjoys spending time with family, cooking, eating good food and traveling. She currently resides in Bethlehem, PA with her spouse and two children.